I0825467

SEATTLE SEAHAWKS

BY MARV ALINAS

The Child's World
childsworld.com

Published by The Child's World®
800-599-READ • childsworld.com

Photography Credits
© AP Photo/Ben VanHouten: 4–5, 7, 12–13; AP Photo/Julio Cortez: 21; AP Photo/Lindsey Wasson: 10–11, 15, 17; AP Photo/Logan Bowles: 19; AP Photo/Stephen Brashear: cover, 2–3; ChrisFloresFoto/Envato: football texture; oasisamuel Shutterstock.com: 6, 9, 15 (football)

ISBN Information
9798895344125 (Reinforced Library Binding)
9798895344132 (Portable Document Format)
9798895344149 (Online Multi-user eBook)
9798895344163 (Electronic Publication)

LCCN 2026935779

Printed in the United States of America

ABOUT THE AUTHOR

Marv Alinas has written dozens of books for children. When she's not reading or writing, Marv enjoys spending time with her family and traveling to interesting places. Marv lives in Minnesota.

Seattle Seahawks wide receiver Jaxon Smith-Njigba

CONTENTS

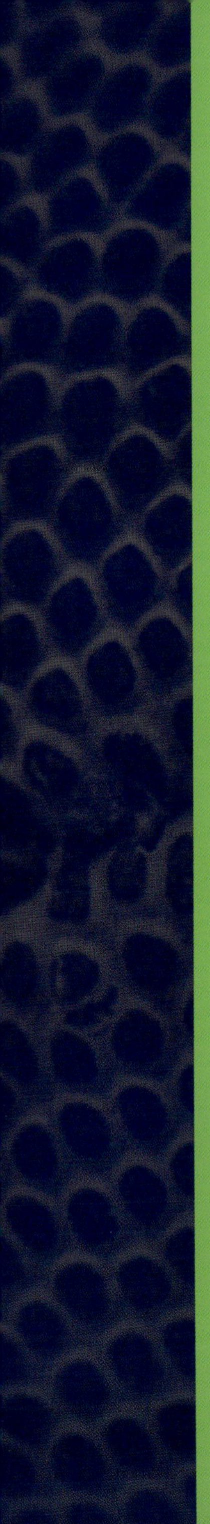

The Team

The Seattle Seahawks are a football team. They play in Seattle, Washington. They started playing in 1976.

The Seattle Seahawks run onto the field to play football.

The Colors

Their team colors are gray, navy blue, and bright green. Their **mascot** is a hawk. His name is Blitz.

The Seahawks also have a live mascot. Taima is an Augur hawk. He flies out of the tunnel ahead of the team on game days.

Blitz has been the Seahawks' mascot since 1998.

The Conference

The Seahawks are in the NFC West. The NFC stands for National Football **Conference**. There are three other teams in the NFC West.

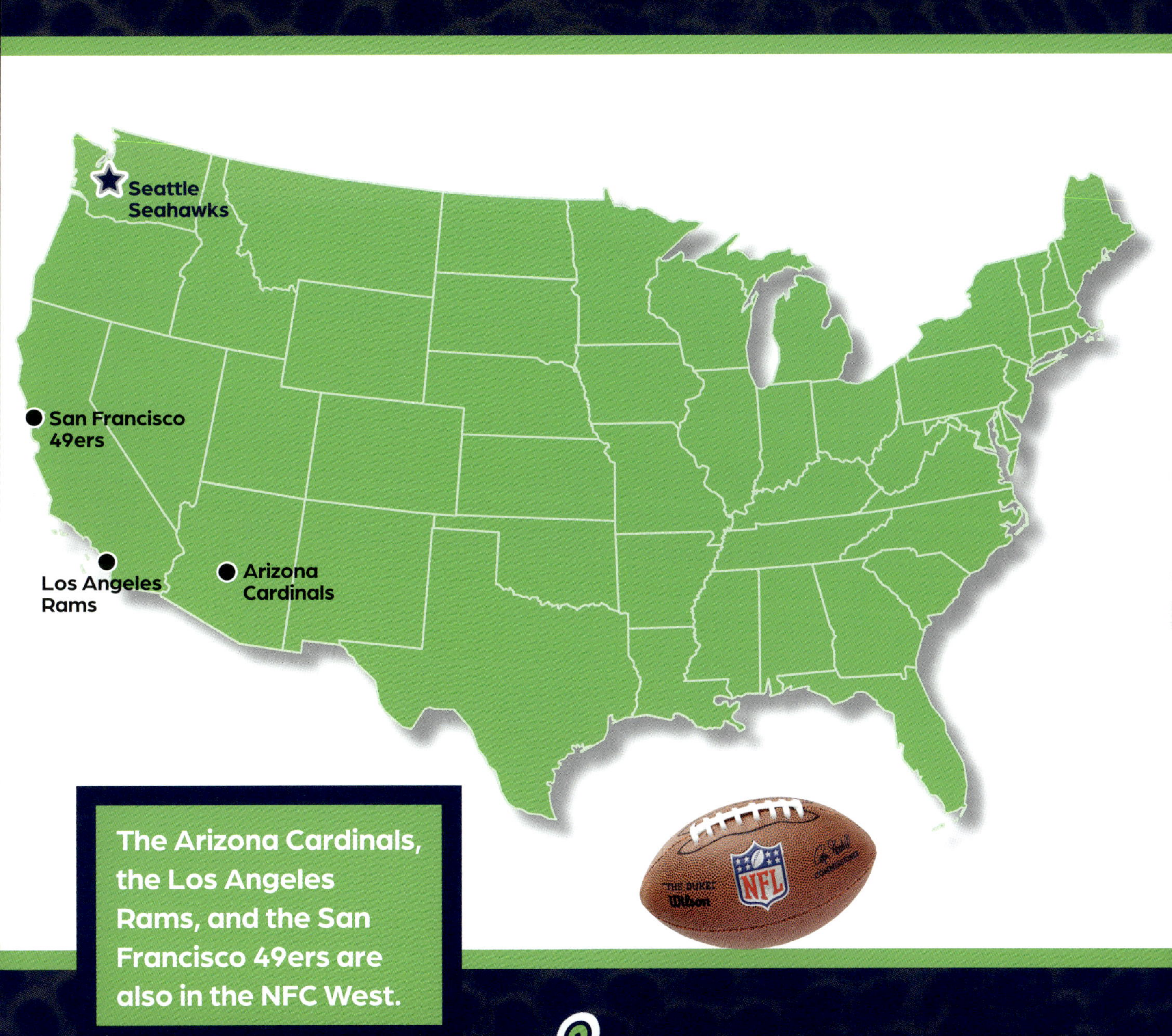

The Arizona Cardinals, the Los Angeles Rams, and the San Francisco 49ers are also in the NFC West.

The Stadium

The Seahawks play at Lumen Field. It opened in 2002. The **stadium** can hold more than 68,000 people.

Lumen Field is one of the loudest stadiums. The roof reflects sound back into the stadium!

The Football Field

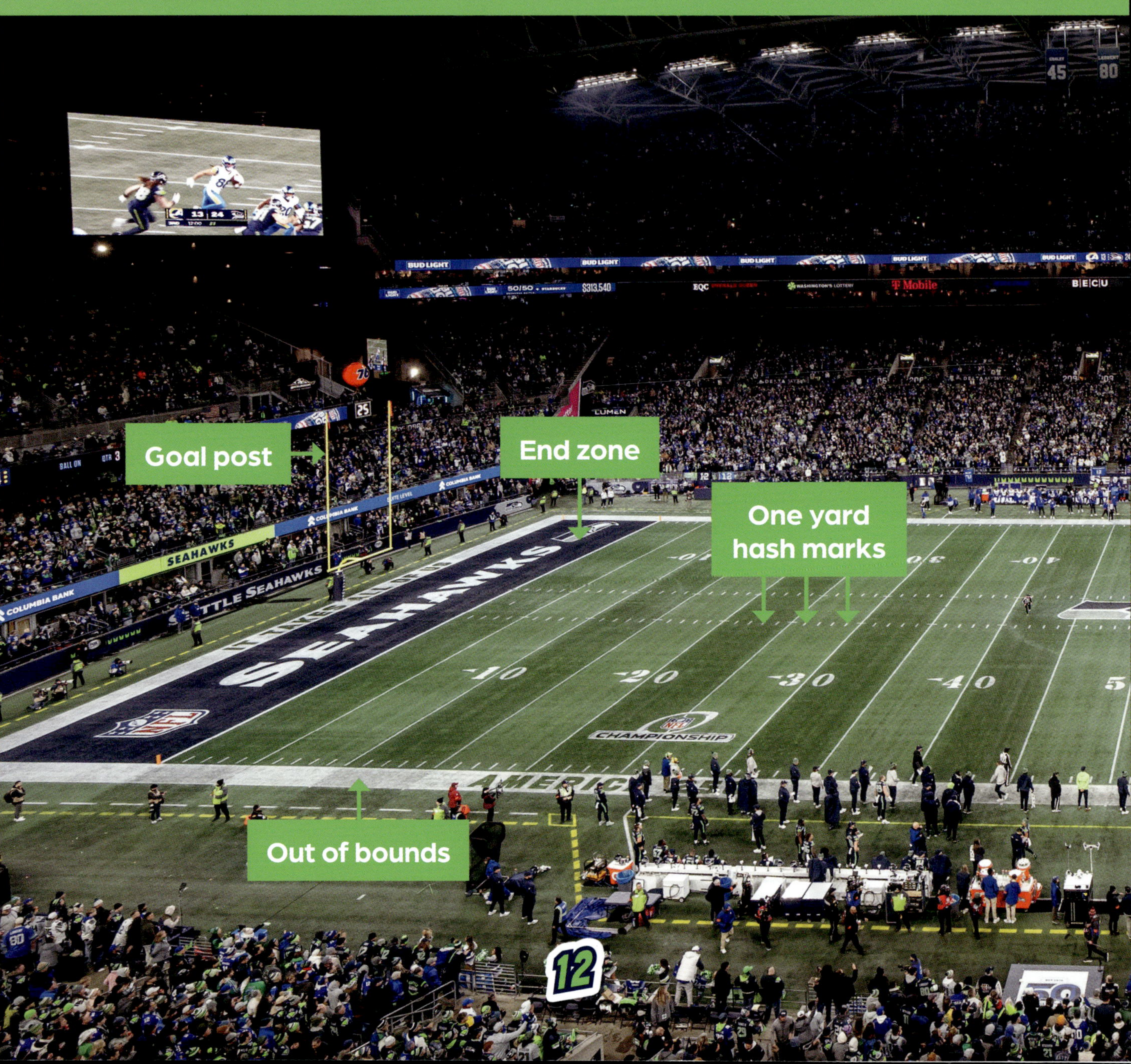

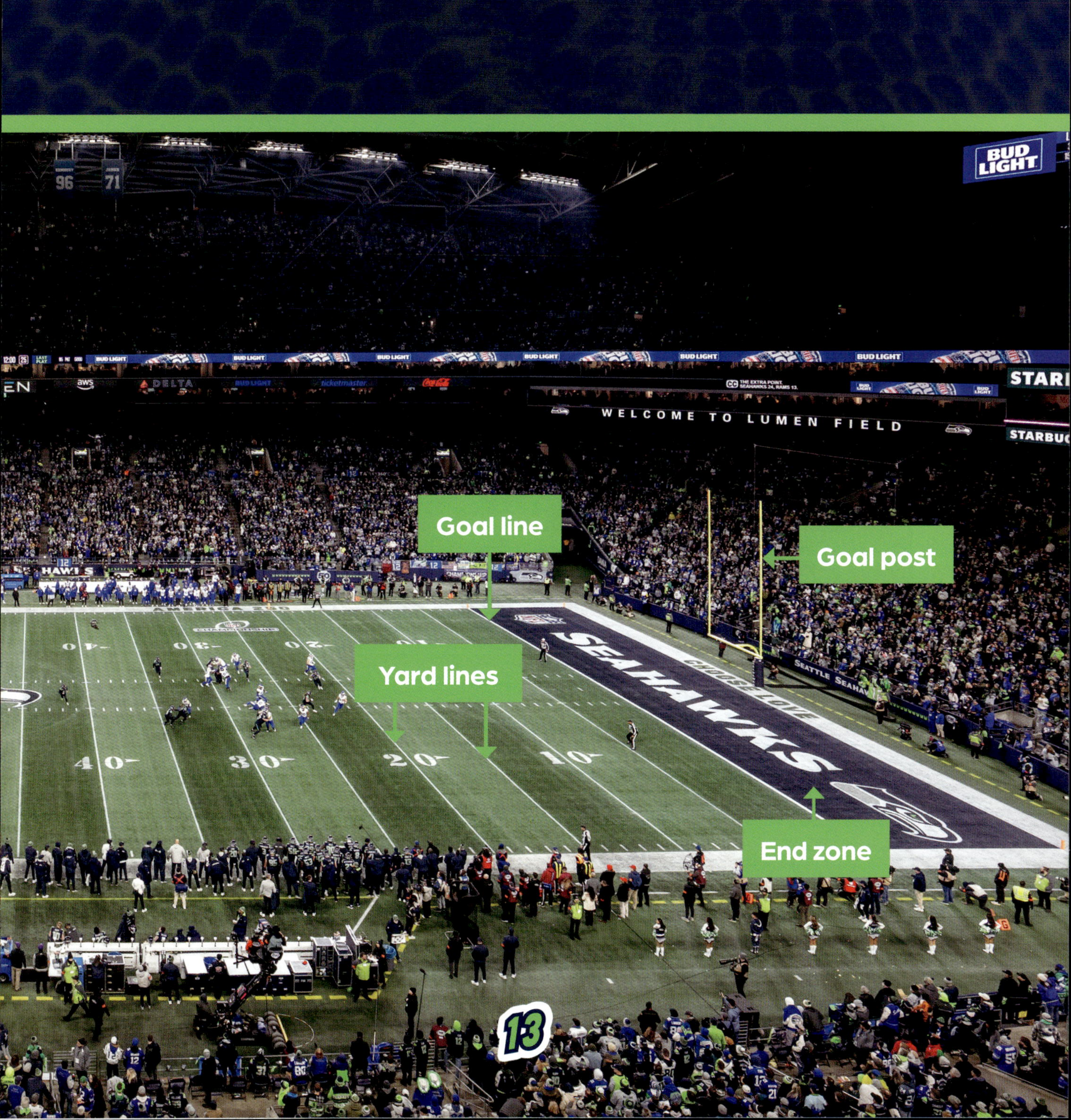

Goal line
Goal post
Yard lines
End zone
WELCOME TO LUMEN FIELD
SEAHAWKS
BUD LIGHT

Fun Fans

Fans of the Seahawks are very loyal and loud. They are known as the "12s." That is because there are 11 players on the football field. The cheering and energy of the fans feels like having an extra player!

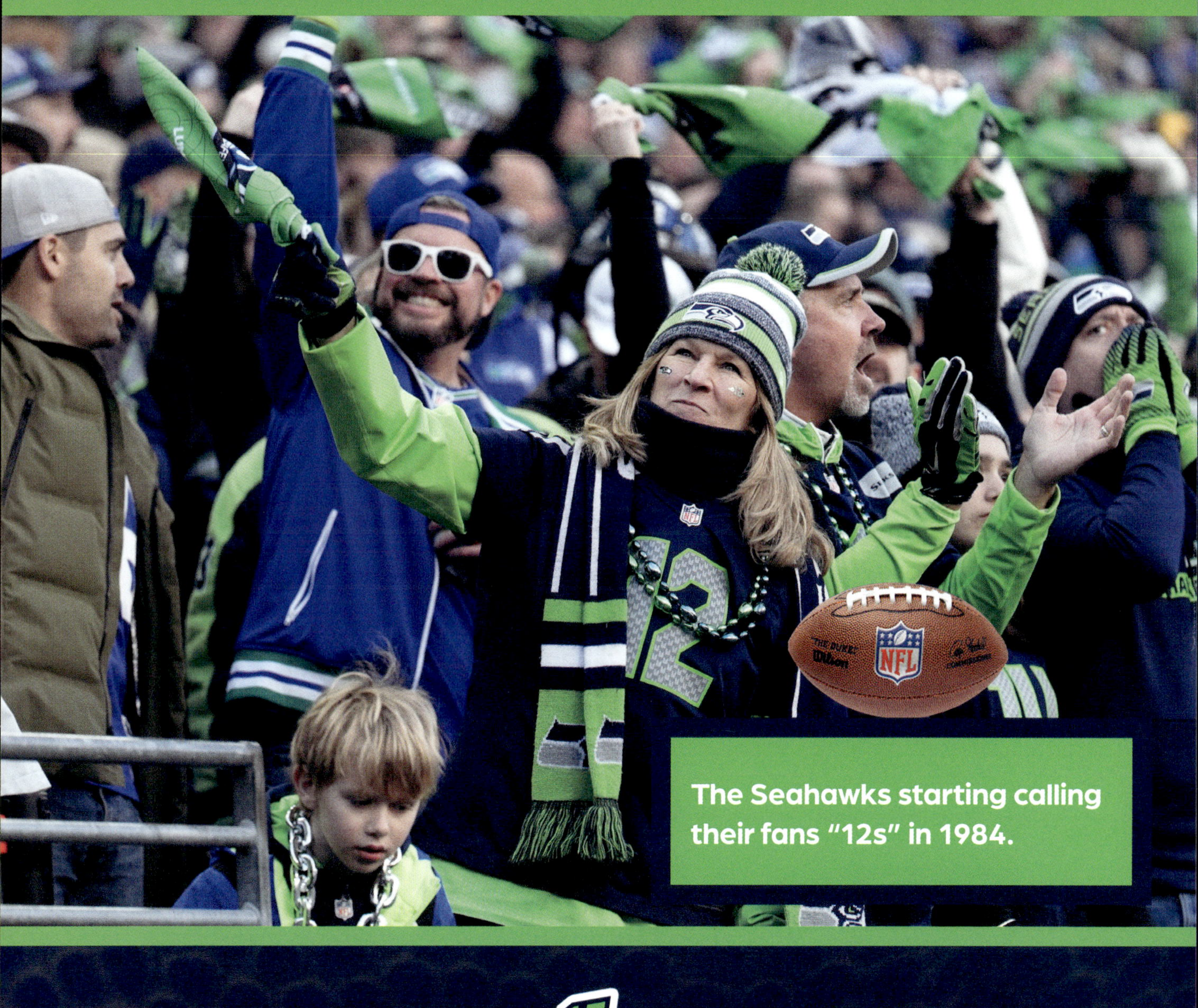

The Seahawks starting calling their fans "12s" in 1984.

The Coaches

The Seattle Seahawks have had 9 head coaches since they began. Mike Macdonald is the current coach. He has been the head coach since 2024.

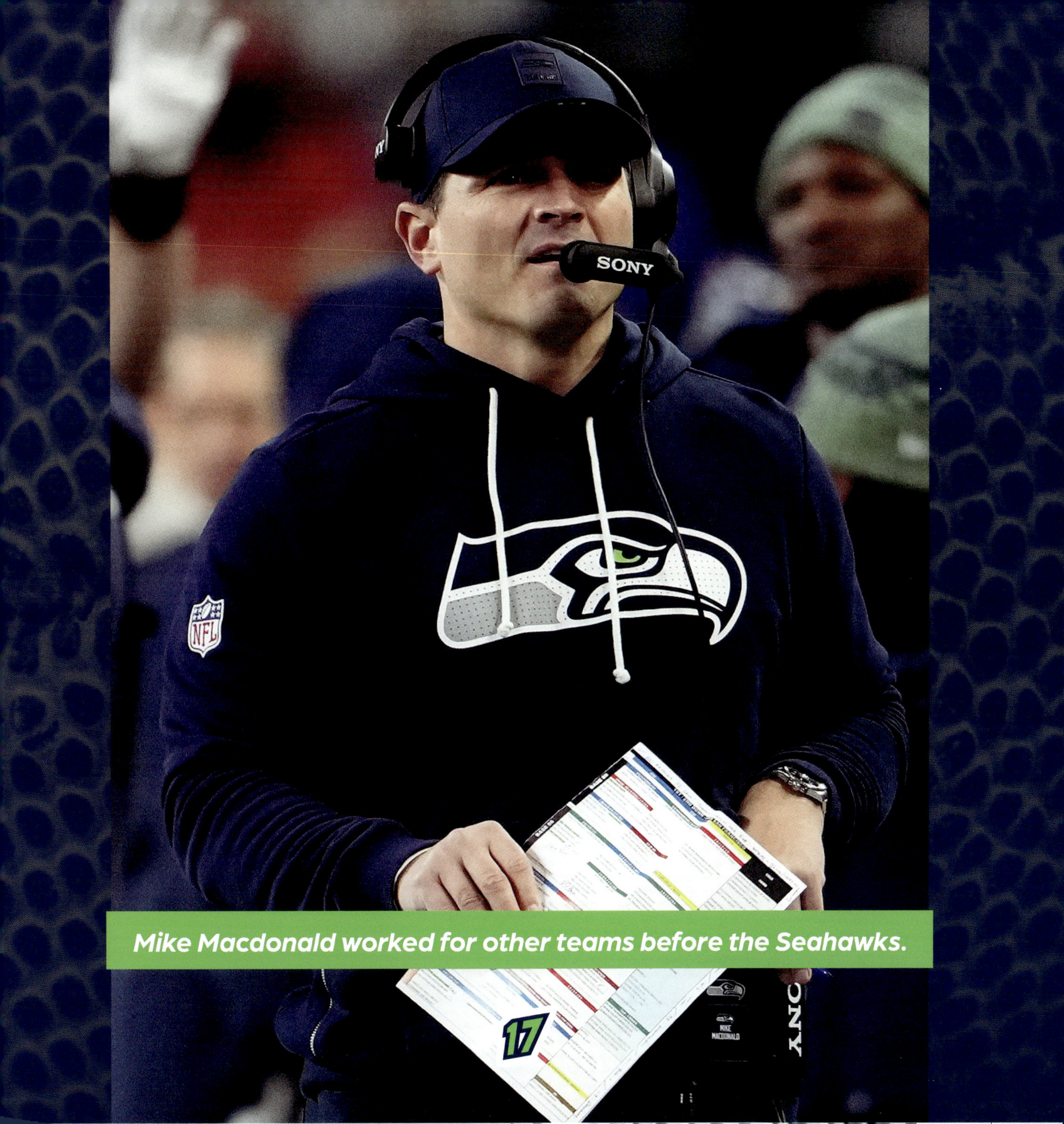

Mike Macdonald worked for other teams before the Seahawks.

The Players

Many great players have been part of the Seattle Seahawks. Some past greats include Walter Jones, Steve Largent, and Cortez Kennedy.

Current Seahawks stars are Jaxon Smith-Njigba and Sam Darnold.

Smith-Njigba and Darnold celebrate after a touchdown.

They are exciting to watch during games.

The Future

The Seahawks have gone to the **Super Bowl** four times. They have won twice. They will keep trying for another win!

The Seahawks last won the Super Bowl in 2026.

FAST FACTS

- The Seattle Seahawks play in Seattle, Washington.
- The team is in the NFC West.
- Lumen Field can hold more than 68,000 people.
- The Seattle Seahawks have won two Super Bowls.

GLOSSARY

conference (KON–fur–enss): In sports, a conference is a grouping of teams.

mascot (MAS–kot): In sports, a mascot is an animal, person, or thing that represents a team.

stadium (STAY–dee–um): A stadium is a large building where sports and concerts are held.

Super Bowl (SOO–pur BOWL): The Super Bowl is the championship game of the NFL.

FIND OUT MORE

In the Library

Anderson, Josh. *Seattle Seahawks.* Parker, CO: The Child's World, 2023.

Klepeis, Alicia. *The Seattle Seahawks.* Minneapolis, MN: Bellwether Media, 2024.

Stewart, Mark. *The Seattle Seahawks.* . Buffalo, NY: Norwood House Press, 2026.

On the Web

Visit our website for links about the Seattle Seahawks:
childsworld.com/links

Note to Parents, Caregivers, Teachers, and Librarians: We routinely verify our web links to make sure they are safe and active sites. So encourage your readers to check them out!

INDEX